MASSACHUSETTS TEST PREP

Practice Test Book

MCAS English Language Arts

Grade 5

ISBN 978-1475132151

CONTENTS

Section 1
Reading Mini-Tests

INTRODUCTION TO THE READING MINI-TESTS
For Parents, Teachers, and Tutors

How Reading is Assessed by the State of Massachusetts

The MCAS English Language Arts (ELA) test assesses reading skills by having students read passages and answer reading comprehension questions about the passages. There are two types of reading questions that students answer on the test. These are described below:

- **Multiple-choice questions** – the majority of the test is made up of multiple-choice questions. Students are given four possible answer choices and must select the correct answer.

- **Open-response questions** – the test contains 5 of these questions. Students are asked a question about a passage and must provide a written answer. Each written answer is 1 to 2 paragraphs longs. Students are expected to show understanding of the text, and are usually required to use relevant information from the text to support their answer.

About the Reading Mini-Tests

This section of the practice test book contains passages and question sets similar to those on the Massachusetts tests. However, students can take mini-tests instead of taking a complete practice test. Each mini-test has one passage for students to read. Students then answer 8 multiple-choice questions about the passage and one open-ended question about the passage.

This section of the book is an effective way for students to build up to taking the full-length test. Students can focus on one passage and a small set of questions at a time. This will build confidence and help students become familiar with answering test questions. Students will gradually develop the skills they need to complete the full-length practice test in Section 3 of this book.

MCAS Reading

Mini-Test 1

Instructions

Read the passage. The passage is followed by questions.

Read each question carefully. Then select the best answer. Fill in the circle for the correct answer.

The last question requires a written answer. Write your answer on the lines provided.

Haunted House

 Marvin refused to believe in ghosts. Even on Halloween, he would not get scared when his friends Steven and Jason shared horror stories. They would gather in his bedroom and sit in pale lamplight talking about ghosts and goblins. The scary stories only made Marvin laugh.

One night they were at Marvin's house enjoying a sleepover. His friends decided to test how scared of ghosts Marvin really was.

"After he has fallen asleep, let's play a trick on him," said his best friend Steven.

"That's a great idea," Jason replied.

Just after midnight, Marvin drifted off to sleep. Steven and Jason looked at each other and nodded. Steven slipped out of his sleeping bag and hid in Marvin's closet. Jason lay still next to his friend and pretended to be asleep. After a moment Steven began to tap gently on the closet door. Marvin stirred gently. Then Steven continued and tapped even harder from behind the door. Marvin sprang from his sleep and sat upright. As the noise continued, he struggled to understand where it was coming from.

"Jason," he whispered. "Do you hear that sound?"

Jason pretended to wake from a deep sleep.

"What's wrong Marvin?" he asked.

"Do you hear that noise?" Marvin asked again.

Jason struggled to keep a smile off his face.

"Yes," Jason replied nervously. "I think it's coming from behind the closet door."

Marvin gulped as fear gripped his body. He climbed from his bed and stepped towards the closet. He began to freeze up as he got closer to the door. His trembling hand reached out towards the handle. Just as he was about to pull the handle, Steven pushed the door open from the other side and shouted loudly. Marvin jumped backwards and fell onto the sleeping bags.

"Do you believe in ghosts now?" Jason asked with a giggle.

Marvin shook his head. Steven was laughing out loud as he sat on a nearby chair. Marvin started to laugh as well.

"Of course he does," Steven said. "But I bet he didn't expect his own house to be haunted!"

1 Read this sentence from the passage.

> **They would gather in his bedroom and sit in pale lamplight talking about ghosts and goblins.**

The word <u>pale</u> shows that the light was –

Ⓐ   bright

Ⓑ   clear

●   dim

Ⓓ   warm

2 Read this sentence from the passage.

> **After a moment Steven began to tap gently on the closet door.**

Which word means the opposite of <u>gently</u>?

●   Softly

Ⓑ   Loudly

Ⓒ   Quickly

Ⓓ   Quietly

3   Which of these happens first in the passage?

Ⓐ   Steven hides in the closet.

Ⓑ   Marvin falls asleep.

Ⓒ   Steven suggests playing a trick.

Ⓓ   Jason asks Marvin if he believes in ghosts.

4   Read this sentence from the passage.

Just after midnight, Marvin drifted off to sleep.

What mood does the phrase "drifted off" create?

Ⓐ   Curious

Ⓑ   Calm

Ⓒ   Playful

Ⓓ   Hopeful

5   Who is the main character in the passage?

Ⓐ   Marvin

Ⓑ   Steven

Ⓒ   Jason

Ⓓ   A ghost

6   Which words does the author use to emphasize how scared Marvin felt?

Ⓐ   "gulped" and "gripped"

Ⓑ   "stepped towards"

Ⓒ   "closer to the door"

Ⓓ   "shouted" and "shook"

7   Why does Marvin most likely jump backwards and fall onto the sleeping bags?

Ⓐ   Steven pushes him.

Ⓑ   Steven scares him.

Ⓒ   He is angry with Steven.

Ⓓ   He wants to go back to sleep.

8   Read this sentence from the passage.

Marvin sprang from his sleep and sat upright.

Why does the author most likely use the word <u>sprang</u> instead of <u>woke</u>?

Ⓐ   To show that Marvin knows about the trick

Ⓑ   To show that Marvin feels sleepy

Ⓒ   To show that Marvin had a bad dream

Ⓓ   To show that Marvin woke suddenly

9 Do you think the trick that Steven and Jason played was mean or funny?

Use details from the passage to support your answer.

I think that the trick Steven and Jason played was mean. Steven woke up suddenly and was starteld. When he got pyshed, I think that that was Mean.

MCAS Reading

Mini-Test 2

Instructions

Read the passage. The passage is followed by questions.

Read each question carefully. Then select the best answer. Fill in the circle for the correct answer.

The last question requires a written answer. Write your answer on the lines provided.

Abraham Lincoln

Abraham Lincoln was the 16th President of the United States. He was born in 1809. He died on April 15, 1865. Lincoln served the United States as President for just short of five years. He is remembered for his strong leadership skills. He led the nation through several conflicts, including the American Civil War.

Abraham Lincoln was born into a poor family. He was mostly self-educated. He worked as a country lawyer. During this period of his life, he also started a family. He raised four children.

His career in politics began at the state level. He was fiercely against slavery. He fought it through national debates. He gave public speeches about the issue. He wrote letters to persuade others to agree with him. His strong opinion won him the support of many. He was then elected president in 1860.

In April 1861, the American Civil War began. Lincoln planned to defeat the South. He wanted to reunify the nation. He oversaw the war effort very closely. He skillfully prevented British support for the South in late 1861. He took control of the civil conflict during the next two years. In 1863, he issued an order that ended slavery. Over 3 million slaves were freed. The war came to an end in 1865. Lincoln achieved his goal of uniting the nation.

Abraham Lincoln was shot and killed just six days after the end of the war. It was a sad end for a man who achieved so much. Abraham Lincoln is thought of by many as the greatest president of all time.

1   Read this sentence from the passage.

He was fiercely against slavery.

As it is used in the sentence, what does the word <u>fiercely</u> mean?

Ⓐ   Usually

Ⓑ   Quickly

Ⓒ   Strongly

Ⓓ   Strangely

2   Read this sentence from the passage.

He wanted to reunify the nation.

If the word <u>unify</u> means "to bring together," what does the word <u>reunify</u> mean?

Ⓐ   To bring together more

Ⓑ   To bring together again

Ⓒ   To stop bringing together

Ⓓ   To bring together before

3   In which year did Abraham Lincoln become president?

Ⓐ   1860

Ⓑ   1861

Ⓒ   1863

Ⓓ   1865

4   The passage is most like –

Ⓐ   a biography

Ⓑ   an autobiography

Ⓒ   a short story

Ⓓ   a news article

5   Which paragraph has the main purpose of describing Abraham Lincoln's achievements during the war?

Ⓐ   Paragraph 1

Ⓑ   Paragraph 2

Ⓒ   Paragraph 4

Ⓓ   Paragraph 5

6   Which sentence from the passage is an opinion?

Ⓐ   *Abraham Lincoln was the 16th President of the United States.*

Ⓑ   *His career in politics began at the state level.*

Ⓒ   *Abraham Lincoln was shot and killed just six days after the end of the war.*

Ⓓ   *It was a sad end for a man who achieved so much.*

7   Which detail about Abraham Lincoln is least important in the passage?

Ⓐ   He became President of the United States.

Ⓑ   He fought to end slavery.

Ⓒ   He was born into a poor family.

Ⓓ   He led America through the Civil War.

8   Complete the web below using information from the passage.

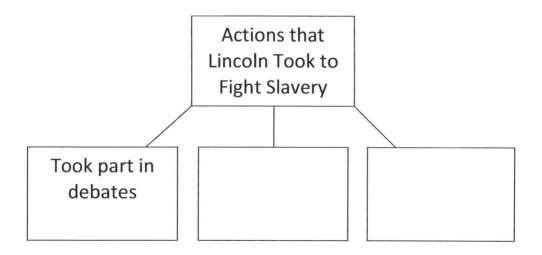

9   The passage describes Abraham Lincoln's achievements. Describe **two** of Lincoln's achievements.

Use details from the passage in your answer.

_____

_____

_____

_____

_____

_____

_____

_____

_____

_____

_____

_____

_____

MCAS Reading

Mini-Test 3

Instructions

Read the passage. The passage is followed by questions.

Read each question carefully. Then select the best answer. Fill in the circle for the correct answer.

The last question requires a written answer. Write your answer on the lines provided.

Keep Smiling

Happiness is something special,
To be enjoyed by young and old,
And then be shared by one another,
To keep us warm through winter's cold.

Whatever time or season,
Or hour of the day,
Happiness can lift your spirits,
More than words could ever say.

And turn your sadness into joy,
Make a smile from a frown.
It brings a burst of gentle laughter,
And lifts you up when you are down.

Without it life is nothing,
Just a pale shade of gray.
An everlasting stretch of nighttime,
That waits patiently for day.

So make the most of living,
And make happiness your friend.
Greet it warmly and keep smiling,
Keep happiness close until your end.

And never doubt its power,
To bring enjoyment out of sorrow,
And leave you smiling though your slumber,
As you wait to greet tomorrow.

1   Read these lines from the poem.

> **And never doubt its power,**
> **To bring enjoyment out of sorrow,**

What does the word <u>sorrow</u> most likely mean?

Ⓐ   Boredom

Ⓑ   Problems

Ⓒ   Sadness

Ⓓ   Peace

2   Read this line from the poem.

> **Happiness can lift your spirits,**

What does this line mean?

Ⓐ   Happiness can be hard to find.

Ⓑ   Happiness can make you feel better.

Ⓒ   Happiness can feel like floating.

Ⓓ   Happiness can bring people closer.

3   The poet describes how life can be "just a pale shade of gray" to show that life can be –

Ⓐ   simple

Ⓑ   weird

Ⓒ   boring

Ⓓ   difficult

4   Read this line from the poem.

It brings a burst of gentle laughter,

Which literary technique does the poet use in this line?

Ⓐ   Alliteration

Ⓑ   Simile

Ⓒ   Metaphor

Ⓓ   Flashback

5   What is the rhyme pattern of each stanza of the poem?

Ⓐ   All the lines rhyme with each other.

Ⓑ   There are two pairs of rhyming lines.

Ⓒ   The second and fourth lines rhyme.

Ⓓ   None of the lines rhyme.

6   What type of poem is "Keep Smiling"?

Ⓐ   Rhyming

Ⓑ   Free verse

Ⓒ   Limerick

Ⓓ   Sonnet

7   Which statement best describes the theme of the poem?

Ⓐ   You should have fun while you are young.

Ⓑ   Every day is a chance to try something new.

Ⓒ   It is important to be happy and enjoy life.

Ⓓ   There is no time like the present.

8   Hyperbole is the use of exaggeration to make a point. Which line from the poem contains hyperbole?

Ⓐ   *To be enjoyed by young and old,*

Ⓑ   *Make a smile from a frown.*

Ⓒ   *An everlasting stretch of nighttime,*

Ⓓ   *As you wait to greet tomorrow.*

9   The poet states that happiness can "keep us warm through winter's cold." Explain what the poet means by this.

_____

_____

_____

_____

_____

_____

_____

_____

_____

_____

_____

_____

MCAS Reading

Mini-Test 4

Instructions

Read the passage. The passage is followed by questions.

Read each question carefully. Then select the best answer. Fill in the circle for the correct answer.

The last question requires a written answer. Write your answer on the lines provided.

Instant Coffee

Coffee is a popular breakfast drink in America for many adults. It comes in numerous varieties. It is produced on several continents worldwide. Adults also often drink coffee when people get together. They chat as they enjoy a nice warm cup. Making a cup of coffee is easy.

Step 1

First you need to boil a kettle full of water. Be sure that the amount of water that you boil is enough to serve all of the people.

Step 2

While the kettle is boiling, take a teaspoon of your favorite coffee and add it to an empty cup. For a stronger taste, feel free to add another half or full spoon of instant coffee to your mug.

Step 3

After you've added your coffee, you can add some sugar if you wish. Many people around the world have their coffee with two teaspoons of sugar. However, some people have more and some have no sweetener at all. It is all about personal taste. If you are making coffee for a group of people, it is a good idea to put a sugar bowl on the table and allow people to add their own sugar.

Step 4

When the kettle has boiled, add the water to your mug. Make sure that you stir the mixture with a teaspoon for approximately 10 seconds.

Step 5

Once it has settled, you can add milk or cream as desired and stir again. Your coffee is now ready to serve!

1   Read this sentence from the passage.

It comes in numerous varieties.

What does the word <u>numerous</u> mean?

Ⓐ   Different

Ⓑ   Tasty

Ⓒ   Many

Ⓓ   New

2   Read this sentence from the passage.

Be sure that the amount of water that you boil is enough to serve all of the people.

Which meaning of the word <u>serve</u> is used in the sentence?

Ⓐ   To help or give assistance

Ⓑ   To offer food or drink

Ⓒ   To work for someone

Ⓓ   To have a use

3   Which sentence from the passage is least relevant to the main idea?

Ⓐ   *Coffee is a popular breakfast drink in America for many adults.*

Ⓑ   *It is produced on several continents worldwide.*

Ⓒ   *Adults also often drink coffee when people get together.*

Ⓓ   *Making a cup of coffee is easy.*

4   What is the main purpose of the passage?

Ⓐ   To teach readers how to do something

Ⓑ   To encourage people to drink more coffee

Ⓒ   To inform readers about the uses of coffee

Ⓓ   To compare different types of coffees

5   If the author was to add a list of items needed to make coffee, which text feature would be best to use?

Ⓐ   Bullet points

Ⓑ   A timeline

Ⓒ   A graph

Ⓓ   Footnotes

6   In which step is milk added to the coffee?

Ⓐ   Step 2

Ⓑ   Step 3

Ⓒ   Step 4

Ⓓ   Step 5

7   The author suggests putting a sugar bowl on the table and allowing people to add their own sugar. What is the main benefit of this?

Ⓐ   The person making the coffee has less work to do.

Ⓑ   It allows people to make their coffee to their own liking.

Ⓒ   It stops people from wasting sugar.

Ⓓ   It prevents the coffee from getting cold.

8   According to the passage, what should you do right after adding water to the mug?

Ⓐ   Add sugar

Ⓑ   Stir the mixture

Ⓒ   Add milk or cream

Ⓓ   Heat the mug

9 Describe **three** ways that people make their coffee unique to them.

Use details from the passage in your answer.

_____

_____

_____

_____

_____

_____

_____

_____

_____

_____

_____

_____

_____

MCAS Reading

Mini-Test 5

Instructions

Read the passage. The passage is followed by questions.

Read each question carefully. Then select the best answer. Fill in the circle for the correct answer.

The last question requires a written answer. Write your answer on the lines provided.

Byron and the Workplace

Byron was set to start work at a new job tomorrow. He only had one day left of his current job. He had found it quite difficult and was looking forward to a fresh start. When Byron began his last day of work, he said good morning to his boss.

Byron's boss was always very moody. His moods seemed to change quickly, and they often caused problems with the staff. Just after lunch, Byron made a mistake while taking some notes from his boss about some new business ideas. His boss stormed over to his desk.

"Typical," Byron's boss said abruptly. "You Librans are all the same."

Byron's boss often referred to people's star signs.

"But I am not a Libran," said Byron. "I am a Scorpio."

Byron had been born on a date that fell right between the two star signs. His boss paused.

"Well, that's good to hear," he replied. "You will need to work on these notes and get them to me by this afternoon though."

Byron quickly fixed up his mistake and his boss settled down. The time came to leave and his day ended well. He left the company with a good reference from his boss and prepared to begin his new job.

After a good night's sleep, Byron got ready for his first day at his new job. He walked into the office and met his new boss. His new boss seemed almost as strange as his old boss. He kept shouting out strange ideas at everyone and he seemed to become upset at the smallest thing. The two of them had a discussion before he started work.

"I noticed you're a Scorpio," his boss said as he shook his head from side to side. "I do not get on well with Scorpios."

Byron paused and smiled.

"Oh, not to worry, sir," he replied. "I am actually a Libran."

His new boss let out a long sigh before walking away.

"Librans are even worse. Get on with it then will you!"

1   Read this sentence from the passage.

Byron quickly fixed up his mistake and his boss settled down.

Which word could best be used in place of <u>settled</u>?

Ⓐ   Sat

Ⓑ   Moved

Ⓒ   Calmed

Ⓓ   Lay

2   Read this sentence from the passage.

His boss stormed over to his desk.

What does the phrase "stormed over" show about Byron's boss?

Ⓐ   He was angry.

Ⓑ   He was tall.

Ⓒ   He walked slowly.

Ⓓ   He spoke loudly.

3   According to the passage, why is Byron able to say that he is different star signs?

    Ⓐ   He does not believe in star signs.

    Ⓑ   He knows that no one knows when his birthday is.

    Ⓒ   He was born right between two star signs.

    Ⓓ   He has a sign for the day he was born and another for the hour.

4   What type of passage is "Byron and the Workplace"?

    Ⓐ   Realistic fiction

    Ⓑ   Science fiction

    Ⓒ   Biography

    Ⓓ   Fable

5   Why does Byron most likely tell his new boss that he is a Libran?

    Ⓐ   He thinks that his boss is a Libran.

    Ⓑ   He thinks it will make his boss like him more.

    Ⓒ   He remembers that his old boss liked Librans.

    Ⓓ   He feels that he is more like a Libran than a Scorpio.

6   Which word best describes Byron's new boss?

    Ⓐ   Agreeable

    Ⓑ   Grumpy

    Ⓒ   Talented

    Ⓓ   Cruel

7   Who is telling the story?

    Ⓐ   Byron

    Ⓑ   Bryon's old boss

    Ⓒ   Byron's new boss

    Ⓓ   Someone not in the story

8   Read these sentences from the passage.

"Typical," Byron's boss said abruptly. "You Librans are all the same."

The word <u>abruptly</u> suggests that Byron's boss sounded –

    Ⓐ   loud

    Ⓑ   confused

    Ⓒ   rude

    Ⓓ   surprised

9   Compare Byron's old boss with Byron's new boss. Include at least **two** ways they are similar in your answer.

Use details from the passage in your answer.

_____

_____

_____

_____

_____

_____

_____

_____

_____

_____

_____

_____

MCAS Reading

Mini-Test 6

Instructions

Read the passage. The passage is followed by questions.

Read each question carefully. Then select the best answer. Fill in the circle for the correct answer.

The last question requires a written answer. Write your answer on the lines provided.

To My Teacher

June 15, 2011

Dear Miss Hooper,

I am writing to thank you for the help you have given me this year. We have covered many subjects in class and you have made sure that I have understood every single one. You explain things so clearly, and are also so patient. Without your assistance, I would of struggled to do as well as I have.

There were so many highlights this year. Whatever the subject, you made it fun and interesting to everyone. All of your students found learning new things so easy because of you. I really believe you have a great skill for teaching others. You should be very proud of the way that you help children to learn. It is because of you that I am thinking about becoming a teacher when I am older.

I have mixed feelings about school next year. Firstly, I guess I am sad that you will no longer be my teacher. However, I am pleased that other children will get to share your knowledge. It would be selfish for me to keep you to myself all through school! I hope that they thank you for the good work that you do. You deserve it and it is the least we can do.

I did not enjoy school much before this year. I was new to the school this year. At my old school, I found learning difficult and quite a challenge. The last nine months have changed all of that. I am now very confident and looking forward to the next school year.

Thank you once again for all of your help. You have truly been a great teacher and helped me greatly. I hope that we may even share the same classroom again one day.

Yours sincerely,

Jacob Maclean

1   Read this sentence from the letter.

There were so many highlights this year.

What does the word <u>highlights</u> refer to?

Ⓐ   The best parts

Ⓑ   Challenges

Ⓒ   Breakthroughs

Ⓓ   Main ideas

2   Which two words from the passage have about the same meaning?

Ⓐ   Help, difficult

Ⓑ   Fun, interesting

Ⓒ   Pleased, glad

Ⓓ   Proud, selfish

3   Which sentence from the passage is a fact?

Ⓐ   *Whatever the subject, you made it fun and interesting to everyone.*

Ⓑ   *I really believe you have a great skill for teaching others.*

Ⓒ   *You should be very proud of the way that you help children to learn.*

Ⓓ   *I was new to the school this year.*

4   What is the main reason Jacob wrote the letter?

Ⓐ   To tell how he wants to become a teacher

Ⓑ   To explain that he is leaving the teacher's class

Ⓒ   To express his thanks to his teacher

Ⓓ   To encourage his teacher to keep working hard

5   Which sentence best summarizes the main idea of the letter?

Ⓐ   *It is because of you that I am thinking about becoming a teacher when I am older.*

Ⓑ   *I have mixed feelings about school next year.*

Ⓒ   *I did not enjoy school much before this year.*

Ⓓ   *You have truly been a great teacher and helped me greatly.*

6   How does Jacob feel about not having Miss Hooper as his teacher next year?

Ⓐ   Upset and angry

Ⓑ   Pleased and excited

Ⓒ   Sad, but understanding

Ⓓ   Confused, but unconcerned

7 Which of these is NOT an effect that Miss Hooper had on Jacob?

Ⓐ Making him look forward to school next year

Ⓑ Making him want to become a teacher

Ⓒ Helping him learn more

Ⓓ Helping him fit in at the new school

8 Look at the chart below.

Why Jacob Thinks Miss Hooper is a Good Teacher

1) She explains things clearly.
2)
3) She makes learning fun.

Which of these best completes the chart?

Ⓐ She is funny.

Ⓑ She is patient.

Ⓒ She is proud.

Ⓓ She is well-trained.

9   Think about a teacher you have had that you appreciated. It could be a school teacher, a coach, or a tutor. Explain what you appreciated most about the teacher.

_____

_____

_____

_____

_____

_____

_____

_____

_____

_____

_____

_____

Section 2
Vocabulary Quizzes

INTRODUCTION TO THE VOCABULARY QUIZZES
For Parents, Teachers, and Tutors

How Vocabulary is Assessed by the State of Massachusetts

The MCAS English Language Arts test includes multiple-choice questions that assess language and vocabulary skills. These questions follow each passage and are mixed in with the reading comprehension questions. Around 12% of the multiple-choice questions on the test are language and vocabulary questions.

Key Vocabulary Skills

There are key vocabulary skills that are focused on in the state tests. The main skills tested on the state test include the following:
- identify word meanings
- analyze word meanings in context
- use words with multiple meanings
- understand shades of meaning
- understand and use suffixes
- understand and use prefixes
- understand and use Greek and Latin roots
- identify antonyms (words that have opposite meanings)
- identify synonyms (words that have the same meaning)

About the Vocabulary Quizzes

This section of the practice test book contains six quizzes. Each quiz tests one vocabulary skill that is covered on the state test. The aim of the quizzes is to help ensure that students have the key vocabulary skills that they will need for the MCAS ELA test.

Quiz 1: Identify Word Meanings

1   What does the word <u>barely</u> mean in the sentence below?

       The cave was so dark that Ken could barely see anything.

    Ⓐ   Only

    Ⓑ   Hardly

    Ⓒ   Empty

    Ⓓ   Scary

2   What does the word <u>peculiar</u> mean in the sentence below?

       Tia worried because Joy had been acting peculiar all week.

    Ⓐ   Odd

    Ⓑ   Mean

    Ⓒ   Normal

    Ⓓ   Friendly

3   What does the word <u>block</u> mean in the sentence below?

       Wayne asked if the trash was going to block the path.

    Ⓐ   A group of buildings

    Ⓑ   A solid piece of something

    Ⓒ   To be in the way

    Ⓓ   To join something to wood

Quiz 1: Identify Word Meanings

4   What does the word <u>gale</u> in the sentence below show?

        Chloe had expected a storm, but not such a gale.

Ⓐ   The storm was over quickly.

Ⓑ   The storm lasted a long time.

Ⓒ   There was a lot of rain.

Ⓓ   There were strong winds.

5   What does the word <u>furious</u> mean in the sentence below?

        I was furious when I found out my computer was broken.

Ⓐ   Worried

Ⓑ   Surprised

Ⓒ   Angry

Ⓓ   Puzzled

6   What does the word <u>produce</u> mean?

        The factory could produce thousands of items each day.

Ⓐ   Find

Ⓑ   Make

Ⓒ   Lose

Ⓓ   Sell

Quiz 2: Analyze Word Meanings

1   If a situation is described as <u>grim</u>, it is —

    Ⓐ   quite unusual

    Ⓑ   easily fixed

    Ⓒ   odd and amusing

    Ⓓ   very serious

2   In which sentence does <u>right</u> mean the same as below?

Chelsea helped because it was the right thing to do.

    Ⓐ   I drove to the end of the street and turned right.

    Ⓑ   James said that we should leave right away.

    Ⓒ   The right to free speech is an important idea.

    Ⓓ   Stella always tries to do what is right.

3   What does the word <u>rock</u> mean in the sentence?

The grandmother liked to rock the baby to sleep.

    Ⓐ   A pebble or stone

    Ⓑ   To affect someone greatly

    Ⓒ   To move from side to side

    Ⓓ   A type of music

Quiz 2: Analyze Word Meanings

4 How is <u>hurling</u> an object different from <u>throwing</u> it?

Ⓐ   The object is thrown straight up.

Ⓑ   The object is thrown with force.

Ⓒ   The object is thrown lightly.

Ⓓ   The object is small and light.

5 Which word can be used to complete both sentences?

Chen used all his _____ to lift the stone.
We _____ meet up later for some lunch.

Ⓐ   strength

Ⓑ   might

Ⓒ   may

Ⓓ   energy

6 Why does the author use the word <u>rushed</u> in the sentence?

The water rushed down the mountain stream.

Ⓐ   To show that the water sounded loud

Ⓑ   To show that the water moved quickly

Ⓒ   To show that the water was clear

Ⓓ   To show that there was only a little water

Quiz 3: Use Synonyms and Antonyms

1 Read the sentence below.

> **Vicky liked how the ice crystals glistened in the sunlight.**

Which word is closest in meaning to <u>glistened</u>?

Ⓐ Melted

Ⓑ Shone

Ⓒ Danced

Ⓓ Warmed

2 Which word means about the same as <u>repair</u>?

Ⓐ Redo

Ⓑ Break

Ⓒ Fix

Ⓓ Change

3 Which two words have about the same meaning?

Ⓐ Ask, answer

Ⓑ Chilly, warm

Ⓒ Dull, dreary

Ⓓ Damp, cold

Quiz 3: Use Synonyms and Antonyms

4 Read the sentence below.

> **Harley always tried to remember his friends' birthdays.**

Which word means the opposite of <u>remember</u>?

Ⓐ   Ignore

Ⓑ   List

Ⓒ   Recall

Ⓓ   Forget

5 Which word means the opposite of <u>wide</u>?

Ⓐ   Low

Ⓑ   Narrow

Ⓒ   Deep

Ⓓ   Thick

6 Which two words have opposite meanings?

Ⓐ   Listen, hear

Ⓑ   Chore, job

Ⓒ   Ache, pain

Ⓓ   Lose, find

Quiz 4: Use Prefixes

1   What does the word <u>preheat</u> mean?

   Ⓐ   Heat more

   Ⓑ   Not heat

   Ⓒ   Heat before

   Ⓓ   Heat again

2   Which prefix can be added to the word <u>print</u> to make a word meaning "print incorrectly"?

   Ⓐ   pre-

   Ⓑ   non-

   Ⓒ   mis-

   Ⓓ   un-

3   Which prefix should be added to the word to make the sentence correct?

Miss Kim ___abled the alarm so she could enter her home.

   Ⓐ   un-

   Ⓑ   dis-

   Ⓒ   in-

   Ⓓ   mis-

Quiz 4: Use Prefixes

4   What does the substance <u>antifreeze</u> most likely do?

ⓐ   Make something freeze quicker

ⓑ   Stop something from freezing

ⓒ   Check to see if something will freeze

ⓓ   Freeze something many times

5   Which prefix can be added to the word <u>just</u> to make a word meaning "not just"?

ⓐ   un-

ⓑ   in-

ⓒ   mis-

ⓓ   dis-

6   Which word contains the prefix <u>re-</u>?

ⓐ   Recipe

ⓑ   Rewrite

ⓒ   Reading

ⓓ   Reason

Quiz 5: Use Suffixes

1 What does the word <u>keenest</u> mean?

Ⓐ Not keen

Ⓑ More keen

Ⓒ The most keen

Ⓓ In a way that is keen

2 Which suffix can be added to the word <u>meaning</u> to make a word meaning "without meaning"?

Ⓐ -less

Ⓑ -ful

Ⓒ -ness

Ⓓ -ly

3 Which suffix should be added to the word to make the sentence correct?

Samuel kind___ asked Sarah if she needed any help.

Ⓐ -ly

Ⓑ -est

Ⓒ -ness

Ⓓ -er

Quiz 5: Use Suffixes

4   What does the word <u>plentiful</u> mean?

   Ⓐ   Having plenty

   Ⓑ   Less plenty

   Ⓒ   More plenty

   Ⓓ   Not plenty

5   Which suffix can be added to the word <u>weed</u> to make a word meaning "full of weeds"?

   Ⓐ   -ness

   Ⓑ   -ing

   Ⓒ   -y

   Ⓓ   -ed

6   In which word is the suffix <u>-est</u> used?

   Ⓐ   Retest

   Ⓑ   Chest

   Ⓒ   Driest

   Ⓓ   Guest

Quiz 6: Use Greek and Latin Roots

1   The word <u>biology</u> contains the Greek root <u>bio-</u>. <u>Biology</u> is probably the study of –

    Ⓐ   life

    Ⓑ   water

    Ⓒ   books

    Ⓓ   people

2   The Latin root <u>jus-</u> is used in the word <u>justice</u>. What does the Latin root <u>jus-</u> mean?

    Ⓐ   Problem

    Ⓑ   Proof

    Ⓒ   Law

    Ⓓ   Person

3   The word <u>periscope</u> is based on the Greek roots <u>peri-</u> and <u>scop-</u>, which mean "around" and "look at." Based on this, what is a <u>periscope</u>?

    Ⓐ   A tool for measuring distance

    Ⓑ   A tool that is easy to find

    Ⓒ   A tool for seeing many different ways

    Ⓓ   A tool that has been studied

Quiz 6: Use Greek and Latin Roots

4   The word <u>centenary</u> contains the Latin root <u>cent-</u>. If a library is celebrating its <u>centenary</u>, it is –

Ⓐ   two years old

Ⓑ   ten years old

Ⓒ   one hundred years old

Ⓓ   one thousand years old

5   The Latin root <u>flor-</u> is used in the word <u>floral</u>. What does the Latin root <u>flor-</u> mean?

Ⓐ   Yellow

Ⓑ   Tiny

Ⓒ   Smell

Ⓓ   Flower

6   The word <u>exoskeleton</u> is based on the Greek root <u>exo-</u>. Based on this, what does <u>exoskeleton</u> mean?

Ⓐ   A skeleton that is on the outside

Ⓑ   A skeleton that is strong

Ⓒ   A skeleton that is inside

Ⓓ   A skeleton that is large

Section 3
MCAS English
Language Arts
Practice Test

INTRODUCTION TO THE MCAS ELA PRACTICE TEST
For Parents, Teachers, and Tutors

How English Language Arts is Assessed by the State of Massachusetts

The MCAS English Language Arts (ELA) test assesses the student's skills by having students read passages and answer questions about the passages. There are two types of reading questions that students answer on the test. These are described below:

- **Multiple-choice questions** – the majority of the test is made up of multiple-choice questions. Students are given four possible answer choices and must select the correct answer.

- **Open-response questions** – the test contains 5 of these questions. Students are asked a question about a passage and must provide a written answer. Each written answer is 1 to 2 paragraphs longs. Students are expected to show understanding of the text, and are usually required to use relevant information from the text to support their answer.

About the MCAS ELA Practice Test

This section of the book contains a practice test just like the real MCAS ELA test. The questions cover all the skills tested on the MCAS ELA test, and include both multiple-choice and open-response questions.

Test Format

The MCAS ELA test is divided into 2 sessions. Students complete one part each day. Students are given 60 minutes to complete each session. You can choose to use this time limit, or you can choose not to time the test.

Students complete the MCAS ELA test by marking their answers on an answer sheet. An optional answer sheet is included in the back of the book.

MCAS English Language Arts

Practice Test

Session 1

Instructions

Read the passages. Each passage is followed by questions.

Read each question carefully. Then select the best answer. Fill in the circle for the correct answer.

Some questions will ask you to provide a written answer. Write your answer in the space provided.

Playing a Musical Instrument

Playing a musical instrument is a popular pastime for all age ranges. Young or old, it is lots of fun to play a musical instrument. There are many different types to choose from including guitar, piano, trumpet, and saxophone.

Making a Choice

First, you need to choose a musical instrument that you would like to learn how to play. Here are some things you should think about:

- the cost of the instrument
- how easy or difficult the instrument is to learn
- whether there is a teacher available to help you learn it
- what opportunities there will be to play it

You might also think about the kind of music you'd like to play. This will probably be the kind of music that you also enjoy listening to.

Getting Your Gear

Now you have chosen your instrument, you need to buy it. If it is expensive, you might like to borrow it instead. That way, you can make sure it is the right choice before spending a lot of money.

Some schools will lend students instruments. Or perhaps you can look in your local paper or online for a secondhand instrument, which are usually much cheaper.

Getting Ready to Learn

After you have your instrument, you should then create a learning plan. This might involve private lessons with a music teacher or going to music classes. Some people choose to learn on their own. You can use books, movies, web sites, or you can even watch videos online.

To learn quickly, your plan may include a variety of learning methods. Make sure that you attend every lesson or study your books regularly. Also, be sure to practice what you have learned as this is the best way to develop your new skill.

Making Music

Once you have learned enough to play a song, you should start playing for people. It is a good idea to start with your family or friends. Or you might play for your music class. Once you become confident, you can then play for larger groups of people.

Keep Going

To become a good musician, you have to keep playing. Keep learning as much as you can and practice often. Challenge yourself to learn more difficult songs as well. As you learn more, you will become better and better. Some people even become good enough to play music as a career.

1   Read this sentence from the passage.

> **Playing a musical instrument is a popular pastime for all age ranges.**

What does the word <u>pastime</u> mean?

Ⓐ   Choice

Ⓑ   Career

Ⓒ   Sport

Ⓓ   Hobby

2   According to the passage, what should you do first?

Ⓐ   Check to see if your school will lend you an instrument

Ⓑ   Decide what instrument you would like to play

Ⓒ   Create a plan for learning to play an instrument

Ⓓ   Look in your local newspaper for an instrument

3   Under which heading is information provided about deciding what type of instrument to learn to play?

Ⓐ   Making a Choice

Ⓑ   Getting Your Gear

Ⓒ   Getting Ready to Learn

Ⓓ   Making Music

4   Read this sentence from the passage.

Keep learning as much as you can and practice often.

Which word means the opposite of <u>often</u>?

Ⓐ   Never

Ⓑ   Rarely

Ⓒ   More

Ⓓ   Regularly

5   The web below lists ways that people can learn to play a musical instrument on their own.

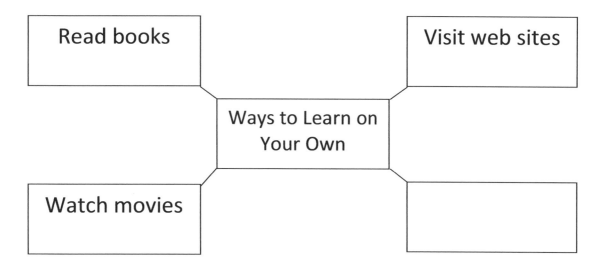

Which of these best completes the web?

Ⓐ   Watch videos online

Ⓑ   Attend a class

Ⓒ   Find a tutor

Ⓓ   Go to concerts

6   What is the main purpose of the passage?

Ⓐ   To tell readers how to do something

Ⓑ   To entertain readers with a story

Ⓒ   To teach people how to play a musical instrument

Ⓓ   To compare different musical instruments

7   Read these sentences from the passage.

> **Once you have learned enough to play a song, you should start playing for people. It is a good idea to start with your family or friends.**

Why does the author most likely suggest starting with your family or friends?

Ⓐ   So your friends will want to learn to play as well

Ⓑ   So your family will see that you are trying hard

Ⓒ   So you do not feel too nervous

Ⓓ   So you can have people join in

8   Why does the author use bullet points in the passage?

Ⓐ   To highlight the main points

Ⓑ   To list a set of ideas

Ⓒ   To show steps to follow in order

Ⓓ   To describe items that are needed

9   If you had to choose a musical instrument to learn to play, which type would you choose? Explain what you considered when making your choice.

Use details from the passage in your answer.

_____

_____

_____

_____

_____

_____

_____

_____

_____

_____

_____

My Shadow
By Robert Louis Stevenson

I have a little shadow that goes in and out with me,
And what can be the use of him is more than I can see.
He is very, very like me from the heels up to the head;
And I see him jump before me, when I jump into my bed.

The funniest thing about him is the way he likes to grow—
Not at all like proper children, which is always very slow;
For he sometimes shoots up taller like an india-rubber ball,
And he sometimes gets so little that there's none of him at all.

He hasn't got a notion of how children ought to play,
And can only make a fool of me in every sort of way.
He stays so close beside me, he's a coward, you can see;
I'd think shame to stick to nursie as that shadow sticks to me!

One morning, very early, before the sun was up,
I rose and found the shining dew on every buttercup;
But my lazy little shadow, like an arrant[1] sleepy-head,
Had stayed at home behind me and was fast asleep in bed.

---

[1] arrant – complete or utter

10 Read this line from the poem.

  He stays so close beside me, he's a coward, you can see;

The word <u>coward</u> is used to show that the shadow is –

Ⓐ   strange

Ⓑ   annoying

Ⓒ   scared

Ⓓ   nearby

11 Which word does the poet use to describe the shadow?

Ⓐ   Shy

Ⓑ   Lazy

Ⓒ   Friendly

Ⓓ   Slim

12 What is the rhyme pattern of each stanza of the poem?

Ⓐ   The second and fourth lines rhyme.

Ⓑ   There are two pairs of rhyming lines.

Ⓒ   The first and last lines rhyme.

Ⓓ   None of the lines rhyme.

13 Which line from the poem contains a simile?

Ⓐ *I have a little shadow that goes in and out with me,*

Ⓑ *And I see him jump before me, when I jump into my bed.*

Ⓒ *For he sometimes shoots up taller like an india-rubber ball,*

Ⓓ *I rose and found the shining dew on every buttercup;*

14 What is the purpose of the footnote?

Ⓐ To give the meaning of a term

Ⓑ To give details of a source

Ⓒ To state the speaker's opinion

Ⓓ To give background information about the poem

15 Read this line from the poem.

He is very, very like me from the heels up to the head;

Which literary device does the poet use in this line?

Ⓐ Simile

Ⓑ Metaphor

Ⓒ Alliteration

Ⓓ Hyperbole

16   What type of poem is "My Shadow"?

Ⓐ   Rhyming

Ⓑ   Free verse

Ⓒ   Limerick

Ⓓ   Sonnet

17   Read this line from the poem.

For he sometimes shoots up taller like an india-rubber ball,

What does the phrase "shoots up" suggest?

Ⓐ   That the shadow grows suddenly

Ⓑ   That the shadow acts strangely

Ⓒ   That the shadow scares the speaker

Ⓓ   That the shadow changes slowly

Manchester United Soccer Club

Manchester United is a famous soccer team. They are based in the United Kingdom. They play in the English Premier League and the European Champions League. They are known as one of the most successful soccer clubs in the world.

They were first formed in 1888. At this time, they were named the Newton Heath Football Club. In 1901, they were sold and were given the new name of Manchester United.

They are the most successful club in the English League. They have won the English Premier League nineteen times. This is one more than their nearest rivals, Liverpool.

Since 1958, Manchester United have also won the European Champions League three times. This competition features teams from across Europe. It is this success that has helped them become such a well-known team.

David Beckham is one of the club's most famous players. He played for Manchester United from 1993 until 2003. In this time, he scored 62 goals for the club and helped his team win eight championships. In 2007, Beckham made an unexpected move. He joined America's Major League Soccer, and began playing for Los Angeles Galaxy. He was paid around $6.5 million per year. One of the most interesting things about the deal was that Beckham was not just paid by the Los Angeles Galaxy team. He was also paid by all the teams in America's Major League Soccer. The teams agreed to this because they hoped that having such a major star in their league would attract more people to the sport.

©Wikimedia Commons

Manchester United's English Premier League Grand Final Wins

Year	Team Defeated
1908	Aston Villa
1911	Aston Villa
1952	Tottenham
1956	Blackpool
1957	Tottenham
1965	Leeds United
1967	Nottingham Forest
1993	Aston Villa
1994	Blackburn Rovers
1996	Newcastle United
1997	Newcastle United
1999	Arsenal
2000	Arsenal
2001	Arsenal
2003	Arsenal
2007	Chelsea
2008	Chelsea
2009	Chelsea
2011	Chelsea

18   Which two words have about the same meaning?

Ⓐ   Famous, well-known

Ⓑ   Formed, named

Ⓒ   Rivals, teams

Ⓓ   Success, competition

19   Which sentence is best supported by the information in the table?

Ⓐ   *They have won the English Premier League nineteen times.*

Ⓑ   *This is one more than their nearest rivals, Liverpool.*

Ⓒ   *Since 1958, Manchester United have also won the European Champions League three times.*

Ⓓ   *This competition features teams from across Europe.*

20   Which sentence from the passage is an opinion?

Ⓐ   *They are based in the United Kingdom.*

Ⓑ   *In 1901, they were sold and were given the new name of Manchester United.*

Ⓒ   *Since 1958, Manchester United have also won the European Champions League three times.*

Ⓓ   *It is this success that has helped them become such a well-known team.*

21   How is the second paragraph mainly organized?

    Ⓐ   A problem is described and then a solution is given.

    Ⓑ   Events are described in the order they occurred.

    Ⓒ   Two teams are compared and contrasted.

    Ⓓ   Facts are given to support an argument.

22   What is the main purpose of the third and fourth paragraphs?

    Ⓐ   To describe how the team formed

    Ⓑ   To describe the team's achievements

    Ⓒ   To explain why the team is successful

    Ⓓ   To show that the team has improved over time

23   Which team has been defeated by Manchester United in the English Premier League final exactly three times?

    Ⓐ   Aston Villa

    Ⓑ   Tottenham

    Ⓒ   Newcastle United

    Ⓓ   Chelsea

24   How does the author show that Manchester United have been a successful team?

Use information from the passage to support your answer.

_____

_____

_____

_____

_____

_____

_____

_____

_____

_____

_____

END OF SESSION 1

MCAS English Language Arts

Practice Test

Session 2

Instructions

Read the passages. Each passage is followed by questions.

Read each question carefully. Then select the best answer. Fill in the circle for the correct answer.

Some questions will ask you to provide a written answer. Write your answer in the space provided.

Trying Too Hard

Robert was determined to do well in his exams. He devoted all of his spare time to study. He had always wanted to be a lawyer when he grew up. He wanted to go to a good college and enjoy a successful career. Unfortunately, this meant that he was almost always serious. Even though he was young, he was unable to relax and enjoy himself most of the time. His friends often got frustrated that he didn't want to spend much time with them.

Robert had an important exam due the following day. He had spent almost an entire week preparing for it. He had managed to get little sleep and was very tired. He even spent the night before the exam revising and had barely managed any sleep at all. However, he thought that he was ready for the exam. He was confident that he had worked harder than anyone else and was sure to get a perfect grade.

After Robert ate his breakfast, he started to feel a little ill. He was tired and unable to focus. He also had a small headache and found it very difficult to concentrate. He still refused to believe that he could ever fail the exam. Robert arrived at the school hall and took his seat beside his friends. He noticed how relaxed and happy they looked compared to him.

"They are just underprepared," he thought to himself as he began his paper.

Despite his best efforts, Robert wasn't able to finish his exam. After twenty minutes, he felt very hot and uncomfortable. He then slumped in his chair, and one of his friends called for help. The school doctor suggested that he was exhausted and would be unable to complete the exam.

He spent the lunch break in the nurse's office. He looked out the window and watched his friends. They smiled and joked and seemed to have not a care in the world. Robert decided that from then on, he wouldn't take it all so seriously.

"I guess I will know better next time," he mumbled.

25   Read this sentence from the passage.

> **His friends often got frustrated that he didn't want to spend much time with them.**

What does the word <u>frustrated</u> mean?

Ⓐ   Worried

Ⓑ   Annoyed

Ⓒ   Confused

Ⓓ   Amused

26   Read this sentence from the passage.

> **"They are just underprepared," he thought to himself as he began his paper.**

What does the word <u>underprepared</u> mean?

Ⓐ   Less prepared

Ⓑ   More prepared

Ⓒ   Not prepared enough

Ⓓ   Too prepared

27   What type of passage is "Trying Too Hard"?

Ⓐ   Biography

Ⓑ   Science fiction

Ⓒ   Realistic fiction

Ⓓ   Fable

28   Which sentence best explains why Robert feels ill during the exam?

Ⓐ   *Robert had an important exam due the following day.*

Ⓑ   *He had spent almost an entire week preparing for it.*

Ⓒ   *He even spent the night before the exam revising and had barely managed any sleep at all.*

Ⓓ   *He was confident that he had worked harder than anyone else and was sure to get a perfect grade.*

29   What happens right after Robert slumps in his chair?

Ⓐ   He keeps working on the exam.

Ⓑ   The nurse comes to see him.

Ⓒ   He starts to feel sick.

Ⓓ   His friend calls for help.

30 Which of these describes the main lesson that Robert learns in the passage?

Ⓐ It is important to have a balanced life.

Ⓑ It is better to have fun than to do well.

Ⓒ Good things come to those who wait.

Ⓓ Friends will be there when you need them.

31 What is the point of view in the passage?

Ⓐ First person

Ⓑ Second person

Ⓒ Third person limited

Ⓓ Third person omniscient

32 What is the organizational structure of this passage?

Ⓐ Chronological order

Ⓑ Main idea and supporting details

Ⓒ Cause and effect

Ⓓ Comparison and contrast

33   At the end of the passage, Robert decides that he shouldn't take things
too seriously. Do you think this is a good decision? Explain why or why not.

_____

_____

_____

_____

_____

_____

_____

_____

_____

_____

_____

_____

The Bees, the Wasps, and the Hornet

 A store of honey had been found in a hollow tree. The wasps stated that it belonged to them. The bees were just as sure that the treasure was theirs. The argument grew very heated. It looked as if the affair could not be settled. But at last, with much good sense, they agreed to let a judge decide the matter. They brought the case before Judge Hornet.

When Judge Hornet called the case, witnesses stated that they had seen certain winged creatures in the neighborhood of the hollow tree. The creatures had hummed loudly, had striped bodies, and were yellow and black.

The wasps stated that this described them. The bees stated that this described them.

This did not help Judge Hornet make a decision. He said he wanted to take a few days to think about the case. When the case came up again, both sides had a large number of witnesses.

Judge Hornet sighed. He knew it was going to be a long day. Then a wise old bee asked if he could address the court.

"I'll allow it," Judge Hornet said.

"Your honor," the bee said, "the case has now been going on for a week. If it is not decided soon, the honey will not be fit for anything. I move that the bees and the wasps be both instructed to build a honey comb. Then we shall soon see to whom the honey really belongs."

The wasps began to panic. They jumped up and down and complained loudly. Wise Judge Hornet quickly understood why they did so.

"It is clear," said Judge Hornet, "who made the comb and who could not have made it. The honey belongs to the bees."

34   The main lesson the wasps learn is about being –

Ⓐ   hardworking

Ⓑ   honest

Ⓒ   prepared

Ⓓ   skilled

35   Read this sentence from the passage.

The argument grew very heated.

The word <u>heated</u> suggests that the bees and wasps became –

Ⓐ   confused

Ⓑ   angry

Ⓒ   warm

Ⓓ   tired

36   Read this sentence from the passage.

The bees were just as sure that the treasure was theirs.

Why does the author most likely use the word <u>treasure</u>?

Ⓐ   To suggest that the honey was gold

Ⓑ   To show that the honey was hidden

Ⓒ   To show that the honey had been there a long time

Ⓓ   To suggest that the honey was precious

37   What is the main purpose of the first paragraph?

Ⓐ   To describe the main problem

Ⓑ   To compare the bees and the wasps

Ⓒ   To introduce the setting

Ⓓ   To describe how to solve an argument

38   How is the passage mainly organized?

Ⓐ   Two events are compared and contrasted.

Ⓑ   Events are described in the order they occur.

Ⓒ   Facts are given to support an argument.

Ⓓ   A question is asked and then answered.

39 Why do the wasps most likely panic when the wise bee suggests that the judge should instruct the bees and wasps to make honey comb?

  Ⓐ The wasps know they cannot make honey comb.

  Ⓑ The wasps are too tired to make honey comb.

  Ⓒ The wasps think the bees' honey comb will taste better.

  Ⓓ The wasps think it will take too long.

40 How are the wasps and the bees similar?

  Ⓐ They can both make honey.

  Ⓑ They are both dishonest.

  Ⓒ They look the same.

  Ⓓ They both panic easily.

41 What type of passage is "The Bees, the Wasps, and the Hornet"?

  Ⓐ Biography

  Ⓑ Historical fiction

  Ⓒ Science fiction

  Ⓓ Fable

42   What is the main problem in the passage? How is the main problem solved?

Use details from the passage to support your answer.

_____

_____

_____

_____

_____

_____

_____

_____

_____

_____

_____

Happy Campers Summer Retreat

As a parent, your child's happiness is the most important thing to you. It is important to keep children healthy and active. This can be difficult to achieve. After all, many people have busy careers as well. The Happy Campers Summer Retreat was developed to help parents with this challenge.

Michael Gibson founded our group in 1998. We run a summer camp for children during the holidays. We are open from May to September. We look after lots of children every single year. The camp is based in the Colorado Mountains. It offers a wide range of activities for children. Our group's mission is to create a new generation of active children across America.

Our program helps improve:
- Physical fitness
- Problem-solving skills
- Social skills
- Sports ability and experience

The Happy Campers Summer Retreat can benefit all children. Some children are good at school, but rarely active. Our program will help encourage an interest in sports. Other children are mainly interested in sports. These children will play sports, but will also learn new skills. Team sports are also very important. They are used to help children develop teamwork skills, social skills, and communication skills. Children will also have the chance to try new activities. Our program is designed to help develop a complete and fully active child.

Our program is very affordable. It is available to any family in America. Your child's stay can be as short as a week or as long as six weeks. We will also cater to any special needs that your child may have.

Why not call us today or send us an email with your enquiry? Take action now and give your child this great opportunity! Our helpful staff will be able to give you all of the answers that you need.

43   Read this sentence from the passage.

Our program is very affordable.

What does the word <u>affordable</u> refer to?

Ⓐ   How easy the program is

Ⓑ   How much the program costs

Ⓒ   How the program benefits children

Ⓓ   How active children need to be

44   Read this sentence from the passage.

The Happy Campers Summer Retreat was developed to help parents with this challenge.

Which word could best be used in place of <u>developed</u>?

Ⓐ   Created

Ⓑ   Changed

Ⓒ   Grown

Ⓓ   Found

45 According to the passage, where is the summer retreat held?

Ⓐ Lake Michigan

Ⓑ Colorado Mountains

Ⓒ Yosemite National Park

Ⓓ Venice Beach

46 Who is the passage mainly written to appeal to?

Ⓐ Parents

Ⓑ Teachers

Ⓒ Students

Ⓓ Sports people

47   Look at the web below.

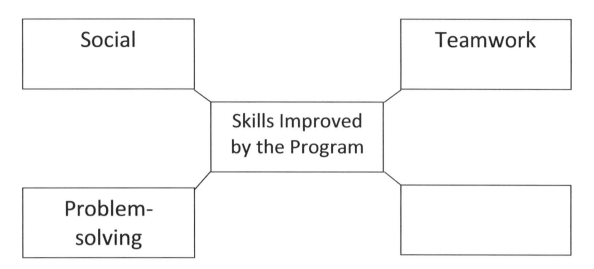

Which of these best completes the web?

Ⓐ   Creative thinking

Ⓑ   Time management

Ⓒ   Communication

Ⓓ   Decision-making

48   The passage was probably written mainly to –

Ⓐ   encourage parents to send their children to the camp

Ⓑ   compare the camp with other activities

Ⓒ   describe the history of the camp

Ⓓ   inform parents about the benefits of outdoor activities

49   Which sentence is included mainly to persuade the reader?

Ⓐ   *After all, many people have busy careers as well.*

Ⓑ   *We run a summer camp for children during the holidays.*

Ⓒ   *It is available to any family in America.*

Ⓓ   *Take action now and give your child this great opportunity!*

50   Which word best describes the tone of the passage?

Ⓐ   Funny

Ⓑ   Concerned

Ⓒ   Positive

Ⓓ   Hopeful

51 Would you like to attend the Happy Campers Summer Retreat? Explain why or why not.

Use details from the passage in your answer.

_____

_____

_____

_____

_____

_____

_____

_____

_____

_____

_____

END OF SESSION 2

Answer Key

The MCAS ELA test given by the state of Massachusetts assesses a specific set of skills. The answer key identifies what skill each question is testing.

The answer key also includes notes on key reading skills that students will need to understand to master the test. Use the notes to review the questions with students so they gain a full understanding of these key reading skills.

Answer Key: Section 1

Mini-Test 1

Haunted House

Question	Answer	Reading Skill
1	C	Use context to determine the meaning of words
2	B	Identify and use antonyms
3	C	Identify the sequence of events
4	B	Identify the mood of a passage*
5	A	Identify the main character of a passage
6	A	Understand and analyze word use
7	B	Understand cause and effect
8	D	Understand and analyze word use
9	See Below	Form an opinion based on a passage and prior knowledge

A complete answer should meet the criteria listed below. Give a score of 0, 1, 2, 3, or 4 based on how well the answer meets the criteria listed.

- It should state an opinion of whether the trick was mean or funny.
- It should use relevant details from the passage to support the opinion.
- It should be well-organized, clear, and easy to understand.

*Key Reading Skill: Mood

The mood of a passage is the way the passage makes the reader feel. It is the atmosphere of the passage. This question is asking what mood is created by a specific phrase. The phrase "drifted off" creates a feeling of calm.

Mini-Test 2

Abraham Lincoln

Question	Answer	Reading Skill
1	C	Use context to determine the meaning of words
2	B	Use prefixes and suffixes to determine the meaning of a word*
3	A	Locate facts and details in a passage
4	A	Identify different types of texts*
5	C	Identify the purpose of specific sections
6	D	Distinguish between fact and opinion*
7	C	Distinguish between important and unimportant details
8	Gave speeches Wrote letters	Summarize information given in a passage
9	See Below	Summarize information given in a passage

A complete answer should meet the criteria listed below. Give a score of 0, 1, 2, 3, or 4 based on how well the answer meets the criteria listed.

- It should provide a clear and accurate description of two of Abraham Lincoln's achievements.
- The achievements identified could be becoming president, ending the civil war, helping to unite the nation, or helping to end slavery.
- It should use relevant details from the passage.
- It should be well-organized, clear, and easy to understand.

*Key Reading Skill: Prefixes and Suffixes

A prefix is a word part that is placed at the start of a word, such as *un-* or *dis-*. The word *reunify* is the base word *unify* with the prefix *re-* added to the start. The meaning of *reunify* is "unify again."

*Key Reading Skill: Identifying Genres (Biography)

A biography is a story of someone's life written by someone other than the person described. This is different to an autobiography, which is the story of someone's life written by that person.

*Key Reading Skill: Fact and Opinion

A fact is a statement that can be proven to be correct. An opinion is a statement that cannot be proven to be correct. An opinion is what somebody thinks about something. The sentence given in answer choice D is an opinion. It describes what the author thinks and cannot be proven to be true. The other sentences are facts.

Mini-Test 3

Keep Smiling

Question	Answer	Reading Skill
1	C	Use context to determine the meaning of words
2	B	Paraphrase content from a passage
3	C	Understand and analyze literary techniques (metaphor)*
4	A	Understand and analyze literary techniques (alliteration)*
5	C	Identify the characteristics of poems
6	A	Identify different types of poems*
7	C	Identify and summarize the theme of a passage
8	C	Understand and analyze literary techniques (hyperbole)*
9	See Below	Identify and explain the meaning of symbolism

A complete answer should meet the criteria listed below. Give a score of 0, 1, 2, 3, or 4 based on how well the answer meets the criteria listed.

- It should provide a clear and accurate explanation of what the statement means.
- The explanation should be related to how happiness can keep people feeling good during difficult times. The student should recognize that keeping warm is not meant literally.
- It should use relevant details from the passage.
- It should be well-organized, clear, and easy to understand.

*Key Reading Skill: Metaphor

A metaphor compares two things, but without using the words "like" or "as." The author uses a metaphor by comparing life without laughter to a pale shade of gray. The metaphor shows how drab and boring life without laughter is.

*Key Reading Skill: Alliteration

Alliteration is a literary technique where consonant sounds are repeated in neighboring words. The words "brings" and "burst" repeat a "b" sound.

*Key Reading Skill: Types of Poems

- A rhyming poem is a poem with a set rhyme pattern.
- A free verse poem does not have a pattern for rhythm or rhyme.
- A limerick is a poem with five lines. The first, second, and last lines rhyme. The third and fourth lines also rhyme.
- A sonnet is a special type of poem with 14 lines and a set rhyme pattern.

*Key Reading Skill: Hyperbole

Hyperbole is a literary technique where exaggeration is used to make a point or emphasize the qualities of something or someone. The phrase "everlasting stretch" is an example of hyperbole.

Mini-Test 4

Instant Coffee

Question	Answer	Reading Skill
1	C	Use context to determine the meaning of words
2	B	Use words with multiple meanings*
3	B	Distinguish between relevant and irrelevant information
4	A	Identify the author's main purpose
5	A	Understand the purpose of text features
6	D	Understand written directions
7	B	Make inferences based on information from a passage
8	B	Identify the sequence of events
9	See Below	Summarize information given in a passage

A complete answer should meet the criteria listed below. Give a score of 0, 1, 2, 3, or 4 based on how well the answer meets the criteria listed.

- It should state three ways that people make their coffee unique.
- The three ways include how much sugar is added, how strong the coffee is, and whether milk or cream is added.
- It should be well-organized, clear, and easy to understand.

*Key Reading Skill: Multiple Meanings

Some words have more than one meaning. These words are known as homonyms. All the answer choices are possible meanings for the word *serve*. The correct answer is the one that states the meaning of the word *serve* as it is used in the sentence.

Mini-Test 5

Byron and the Workplace

Question	Answer	Reading Skill
1	C	Identify and use synonyms
2	A	Identify the meaning of phrases
3	C	Locate facts and details in a passage
4	A	Identify different types of texts*
5	B	Make inferences about characters
6	B	Draw conclusions about characters
7	D	Identify point of view
8	C	Understand and analyze word use
9	See Below	Compare and contrast characters

A complete answer should meet the criteria listed below. Give a score of 0, 1, 2, 3, or 4 based on how well the answer meets the criteria listed.

- It should provide a clear and accurate explanation of at least two ways that the two bosses are similar.
- The similarities could include that they both seem moody or grumpy, that they both seem rude or difficult to get along with, and that they both refer to star signs.
- It should use relevant details from the passage.
- It should be well-organized, clear, and easy to understand.

*Key Reading Skill: Identifying Genres (Realistic Fiction)

Realistic fiction refers to fiction that describes events that could really happen. The passage is still fictional, or made-up. However, the events described could actually happen to someone.

Mini-Test 6

To My Teacher

Question	Answer	Reading Skill
1	A	Use context to determine the meaning of words
2	C	Identify and use synonyms
3	D	Distinguish between fact and opinion*
4	C	Identify the author's main purpose
5	D	Identify the main idea
6	C	Make inferences about characters
7	D	Locate facts and details in a passage
8	B	Summarize information given in a passage
9	See Below	Use prior knowledge to relate to a passage

A complete answer should meet the criteria listed below. Give a score of 0, 1, 2, 3, or 4 based on how well the answer meets the criteria listed.

- It should provide a description of a teacher that the student appreciated.
- It should clearly explain what the student appreciated about the teacher.
- It should be well-organized, clear, and easy to understand.

*Key Reading Skill: Fact and Opinion

A fact is a statement that can be proven to be correct. An opinion is a statement that cannot be proven to be correct. The sentence given in answer choice D is a fact. The other statements are all opinions of the author.

Answer Key: Section 2

Quiz 1: Identify Word Meanings

Question	Answer
1	B
2	A
3	C
4	D
5	C
6	B

Quiz 2: Analyze Word Meanings

Question	Answer
1	D
2	D
3	C
4	B
5	B
6	B

Quiz 3: Use Synonyms and Antonyms

Question	Answer
1	B
2	C
3	C
4	D
5	B
6	D

Quiz 4: Use Prefixes

Question	Answer
1	C
2	C
3	B
4	B
5	A
6	B

Quiz 5: Use Suffixes

Question	Answer
1	C
2	A
3	A
4	A
5	C
6	C

Quiz 6: Use Greek and Latin Roots

Question	Answer
1	A
2	C
3	C
4	C
5	D
6	A

Answer Key: Section 3

MCAS English Language Arts Practice Test: Session 1

Question	Answer	Reading Skill
1	D	Use context to determine the meaning of words
2	B	Identify the sequence of events
3	A	Identify the purpose of specific sections
4	B	Identify and use antonyms
5	A	Summarize information given in a passage
6	A	Identify the author's purpose
7	C	Make inferences based on information from a passage
8	B	Identify the purpose of text features
9	See Below	Form an opinion based on a passage
10	C	Use context to determine the meaning of words
11	B	Locate facts and details in a passage
12	B	Identify the characteristics of poems
13	C	Understand and analyze literary techniques (simile)*
14	A	Identify the purpose of text features
15	C	Understand and analyze literary techniques (alliteration)*
16	A	Identify different types of poems*
17	A	Understand and analyze word use
18	A	Identify and use synonyms
19	A	Understand information in graphs, charts, or tables
20	D	Distinguish between fact and opinion*
21	B	Identify how a passage is organized
22	B	Identify the author's main purpose
23	A	Understand information in graphs, charts, or tables
24	See Below	Identify details that support a conclusion

Q9.

A complete answer should meet the criteria listed below. Give a score of 0, 1, 2, 3, or 4 based on how well the answer meets the criteria listed.

- It should state which musical instrument the student would choose.
- It should provide a fully-supported explanation of why the student made that choice.
- It should use relevant details from the passage, such as the advice the author gives on what to consider when choosing a musical instrument.
- It should be well-organized, clear, and easy to understand.

Q24.

A complete answer should meet the criteria listed below. Give a score of 0, 1, 2, 3, or 4 based on how well the answer meets the criteria listed.

- It should give details that show that Manchester United have been a successful team.
- The details may include that the team has won the English Premier League nineteen times, that the team has won the English Premier League more times than any other team, and that the team has won the European Champions League three times.
- It should be well-organized, clear, and easy to understand.

*Key Reading Skills

Q13: Simile

A simile compares two things using the words "like" or "as." The phrase "like an india-rubber ball" is an example of a simile.

Q15: Alliteration

Alliteration is a literary technique where consonant sounds are repeated in neighboring words. The phrase "heels up to the head" uses alliteration because of the repeated "h" sound.

Q16: Types of Poems

- A rhyming poem is a poem with a set rhyme pattern.
- A free verse poem is a poem that does not have a pattern for rhythm or rhyme.
- A limerick is a poem with five lines. The first, second, and last lines rhyme. The third and fourth lines also rhyme.
- A sonnet is a special type of poem with 14 lines and a set rhyme pattern.

The poem rhymes, but does not have the structure of a limerick or a sonnet. The poem is best described as a rhyming poem.

Q20: Fact and Opinion

A fact is a statement that can be proven to be correct. An opinion is a statement that cannot be proven to be correct. The sentence given in answer choice D is an opinion. It cannot be proven to be correct.

MCAS English Language Arts Practice Test: Session 2

Question	Answer	Reading Skill
25	B	Use context to determine the meaning of words
26	C	Use word parts to determine the meaning of words
27	C	Identify different types of texts*
28	C	Understand cause and effect
29	D	Identify the sequence of events
30	A	Identify and summarize the theme of a passage
31	D	Identify point of view*
32	A	Identify how a passage is organized
33	See Below	Form an opinion based on a passage and prior knowledge
34	B	Identify and summarize the theme of a passage
35	B	Use context to determine word meaning
36	D	Understand and analyze word use
37	A	Identify the purpose of specific sections
38	B	Identify how a passage is organized
39	A	Make inferences based on information in a passage
40	C	Compare and contrast two items
41	D	Identify different types of texts*
42	See Below	Understand and analyze the plot of a passage
43	B	Identify word meaning
44	A	Identify and use synonyms
45	B	Locate facts and details in a passage
46	A	Infer the intended audience of a passage
47	C	Summarize information given in a passage
48	A	Identify the author's main purpose
49	D	Identify the purpose of specific information
50	C	Identify the tone of a passage*
51	See Below	Form an opinion based on a passage

Q33.

A complete answer should meet the criteria listed below. Give a score of 0, 1, 2, 3, or 4 based on how well the answer meets the criteria listed.

- It should explain whether the student believes that Robert's decision to be more serious was a good decision.
- It should provide a fully-supported explanation of why or why not.
- It should use relevant details from the passage.
- It should be well-organized, clear, and easy to understand.

Q42.

A complete answer should meet the criteria listed below. Give a score of 0, 1, 2, 3, or 4 based on how well the answer meets the criteria listed.

- It should describe the main problem as being that nobody can tell whether the honey belongs to the wasps or the bees.
- It should clearly explain how the problem is resolved.
- This should refer to how the judge tells the wasps and bees to make honey, and realizes by how the wasps respond that they are unable to make honey.
- It should be well-organized, clear, and easy to understand.

Q51.

A complete answer should meet the criteria listed below. Give a score of 0, 1, 2, 3, or 4 based on how well the answer meets the criteria listed.

- It should state whether or not the student would like to attend the retreat.
- It should provide a fully-supported explanation of why or why not.
- It should use relevant details from the passage.
- It should be well-organized, clear, and easy to understand.

*Key Reading Skills

Q27: Identifying Genres (Realistic Fiction)

Realistic fiction refers to fiction that describes events that could really happen. The passage is still fictional, or made-up. However, the events described could actually happen to someone.

Q31: Point of View

This question is asking about the point of view of the passage. The point of view of the passage is third person omniscient. It is told by a person outside the story that knows everything about the characters.

Q41: Identifying Genres (Fable)

A fable is a story that has the main purpose of teaching a moral lesson. Fables usually have animals as characters.

Q50: Tone

The tone of a passage refers to the author's attitude. It is how the author feels about the content of the passage. For example, the tone could be serious, sad, cheerful, or witty. In this case, the tone is positive.

Answer Sheet: Section 1

Mini-Test 1	Mini-Test 2	Mini-Test 3
1 Ⓐ Ⓑ Ⓒ Ⓓ	1 Ⓐ Ⓑ Ⓒ Ⓓ	1 Ⓐ Ⓑ Ⓒ Ⓓ
2 Ⓐ Ⓑ Ⓒ Ⓓ	2 Ⓐ Ⓑ Ⓒ Ⓓ	2 Ⓐ Ⓑ Ⓒ Ⓓ
3 Ⓐ Ⓑ Ⓒ Ⓓ	3 Ⓐ Ⓑ Ⓒ Ⓓ	3 Ⓐ Ⓑ Ⓒ Ⓓ
4 Ⓐ Ⓑ Ⓒ Ⓓ	4 Ⓐ Ⓑ Ⓒ Ⓓ	4 Ⓐ Ⓑ Ⓒ Ⓓ
5 Ⓐ Ⓑ Ⓒ Ⓓ	5 Ⓐ Ⓑ Ⓒ Ⓓ	5 Ⓐ Ⓑ Ⓒ Ⓓ
6 Ⓐ Ⓑ Ⓒ Ⓓ	6 Ⓐ Ⓑ Ⓒ Ⓓ	6 Ⓐ Ⓑ Ⓒ Ⓓ
7 Ⓐ Ⓑ Ⓒ Ⓓ	7 Ⓐ Ⓑ Ⓒ Ⓓ	7 Ⓐ Ⓑ Ⓒ Ⓓ
8 Ⓐ Ⓑ Ⓒ Ⓓ	8 Ⓐ Ⓑ Ⓒ Ⓓ	8 Ⓐ Ⓑ Ⓒ Ⓓ

Answer Sheet: Section 1

Mini-Test 4	Mini-Test 5	Mini-Test 6
1 Ⓐ Ⓑ Ⓒ Ⓓ	1 Ⓐ Ⓑ Ⓒ Ⓓ	1 Ⓐ Ⓑ Ⓒ Ⓓ
2 Ⓐ Ⓑ Ⓒ Ⓓ	2 Ⓐ Ⓑ Ⓒ Ⓓ	2 Ⓐ Ⓑ Ⓒ Ⓓ
3 Ⓐ Ⓑ Ⓒ Ⓓ	3 Ⓐ Ⓑ Ⓒ Ⓓ	3 Ⓐ Ⓑ Ⓒ Ⓓ
4 Ⓐ Ⓑ Ⓒ Ⓓ	4 Ⓐ Ⓑ Ⓒ Ⓓ	4 Ⓐ Ⓑ Ⓒ Ⓓ
5 Ⓐ Ⓑ Ⓒ Ⓓ	5 Ⓐ Ⓑ Ⓒ Ⓓ	5 Ⓐ Ⓑ Ⓒ Ⓓ
6 Ⓐ Ⓑ Ⓒ Ⓓ	6 Ⓐ Ⓑ Ⓒ Ⓓ	6 Ⓐ Ⓑ Ⓒ Ⓓ
7 Ⓐ Ⓑ Ⓒ Ⓓ	7 Ⓐ Ⓑ Ⓒ Ⓓ	7 Ⓐ Ⓑ Ⓒ Ⓓ
8 Ⓐ Ⓑ Ⓒ Ⓓ	8 Ⓐ Ⓑ Ⓒ Ⓓ	8 Ⓐ Ⓑ Ⓒ Ⓓ

Answer Sheet: Section 2

Quiz 1		Quiz 2		Quiz 3	
1	Ⓐ Ⓑ Ⓒ Ⓓ	1	Ⓐ Ⓑ Ⓒ Ⓓ	1	Ⓐ Ⓑ Ⓒ Ⓓ
2	Ⓐ Ⓑ Ⓒ Ⓓ	2	Ⓐ Ⓑ Ⓒ Ⓓ	2	Ⓐ Ⓑ Ⓒ Ⓓ
3	Ⓐ Ⓑ Ⓒ Ⓓ	3	Ⓐ Ⓑ Ⓒ Ⓓ	3	Ⓐ Ⓑ Ⓒ Ⓓ
4	Ⓐ Ⓑ Ⓒ Ⓓ	4	Ⓐ Ⓑ Ⓒ Ⓓ	4	Ⓐ Ⓑ Ⓒ Ⓓ
5	Ⓐ Ⓑ Ⓒ Ⓓ	5	Ⓐ Ⓑ Ⓒ Ⓓ	5	Ⓐ Ⓑ Ⓒ Ⓓ
6	Ⓐ Ⓑ Ⓒ Ⓓ	6	Ⓐ Ⓑ Ⓒ Ⓓ	6	Ⓐ Ⓑ Ⓒ Ⓓ

Quiz 4		Quiz 5		Quiz 6	
1	Ⓐ Ⓑ Ⓒ Ⓓ	1	Ⓐ Ⓑ Ⓒ Ⓓ	1	Ⓐ Ⓑ Ⓒ Ⓓ
2	Ⓐ Ⓑ Ⓒ Ⓓ	2	Ⓐ Ⓑ Ⓒ Ⓓ	2	Ⓐ Ⓑ Ⓒ Ⓓ
3	Ⓐ Ⓑ Ⓒ Ⓓ	3	Ⓐ Ⓑ Ⓒ Ⓓ	3	Ⓐ Ⓑ Ⓒ Ⓓ
4	Ⓐ Ⓑ Ⓒ Ⓓ	4	Ⓐ Ⓑ Ⓒ Ⓓ	4	Ⓐ Ⓑ Ⓒ Ⓓ
5	Ⓐ Ⓑ Ⓒ Ⓓ	5	Ⓐ Ⓑ Ⓒ Ⓓ	5	Ⓐ Ⓑ Ⓒ Ⓓ
6	Ⓐ Ⓑ Ⓒ Ⓓ	6	Ⓐ Ⓑ Ⓒ Ⓓ	6	Ⓐ Ⓑ Ⓒ Ⓓ

Answer Sheet: Section 3

MCAS ELA Practice Test: Session 1					
1	Ⓐ Ⓑ Ⓒ Ⓓ	9	O/R	17	Ⓐ Ⓑ Ⓒ Ⓓ
2	Ⓐ Ⓑ Ⓒ Ⓓ	10	Ⓐ Ⓑ Ⓒ Ⓓ	18	Ⓐ Ⓑ Ⓒ Ⓓ
3	Ⓐ Ⓑ Ⓒ Ⓓ	11	Ⓐ Ⓑ Ⓒ Ⓓ	19	Ⓐ Ⓑ Ⓒ Ⓓ
4	Ⓐ Ⓑ Ⓒ Ⓓ	12	Ⓐ Ⓑ Ⓒ Ⓓ	20	Ⓐ Ⓑ Ⓒ Ⓓ
5	Ⓐ Ⓑ Ⓒ Ⓓ	13	Ⓐ Ⓑ Ⓒ Ⓓ	21	Ⓐ Ⓑ Ⓒ Ⓓ
6	Ⓐ Ⓑ Ⓒ Ⓓ	14	Ⓐ Ⓑ Ⓒ Ⓓ	22	Ⓐ Ⓑ Ⓒ Ⓓ
7	Ⓐ Ⓑ Ⓒ Ⓓ	15	Ⓐ Ⓑ Ⓒ Ⓓ	23	Ⓐ Ⓑ Ⓒ Ⓓ
8	Ⓐ Ⓑ Ⓒ Ⓓ	16	Ⓐ Ⓑ Ⓒ Ⓓ	24	O/R

Answer Sheet: Section 3

MCAS ELA Practice Test: Session 2

25	Ⓐ Ⓑ Ⓒ Ⓓ	35	Ⓐ Ⓑ Ⓒ Ⓓ	45	Ⓐ Ⓑ Ⓒ Ⓓ
26	Ⓐ Ⓑ Ⓒ Ⓓ	36	Ⓐ Ⓑ Ⓒ Ⓓ	46	Ⓐ Ⓑ Ⓒ Ⓓ
27	Ⓐ Ⓑ Ⓒ Ⓓ	37	Ⓐ Ⓑ Ⓒ Ⓓ	47	Ⓐ Ⓑ Ⓒ Ⓓ
28	Ⓐ Ⓑ Ⓒ Ⓓ	38	Ⓐ Ⓑ Ⓒ Ⓓ	48	Ⓐ Ⓑ Ⓒ Ⓓ
29	Ⓐ Ⓑ Ⓒ Ⓓ	39	Ⓐ Ⓑ Ⓒ Ⓓ	49	Ⓐ Ⓑ Ⓒ Ⓓ
30	Ⓐ Ⓑ Ⓒ Ⓓ	40	Ⓐ Ⓑ Ⓒ Ⓓ	50	Ⓐ Ⓑ Ⓒ Ⓓ
31	Ⓐ Ⓑ Ⓒ Ⓓ	41	Ⓐ Ⓑ Ⓒ Ⓓ	51	O/R
32	Ⓐ Ⓑ Ⓒ Ⓓ	42	O/R		
33	O/R	43	Ⓐ Ⓑ Ⓒ Ⓓ		
34	Ⓐ Ⓑ Ⓒ Ⓓ	44	Ⓐ Ⓑ Ⓒ Ⓓ		

Massachusetts Test Prep Writing Workbook

For help with the writing section of the MCAS English Language Arts test, get the Massachusetts Test Prep Writing Workbook. It contains reading comprehension writing tasks, guided writing tasks, and practice writing prompts.

Made in the USA
Lexington, KY
20 December 2012